The 3 B's That Do Not Sting

The Three-Step Process to Christian Discipleship

Ronnie D. Simmons

The 3 B's That Do Not Sting

Copyright © 2023 by Ronnie D. Simmons. All rights reserved

Cover Design by Alpha Advertising, Michael Cox

The scanning, uploading, and distribution of this book without permission is a theft of intellectual property. If you would like permission to use material from this book (other than for review purposes) kindly contact the author at rdsimmons2@att.net.

Ronnie D. Simmons Ministries
P.O. Box 985
Smyrna TN 37167615-223-0420
www.houseoffaithchristiancenter.org First edition: Softcover (September 2023)

Unless otherwise noted, Scripture quotations are taken from the Holy Bible, King James Version, New King James Version, English Standard Version, and New Living Standard
Scripture quotations are taken from The Holy Bible, New International Version® NIV®

Copyright © 1973, 1978, 1984, 2011 by Biblica, Inc. Used with permission. All rights reserved worldwide. | "Scripture quotations are from the ESV® Bible (The Holy Bible, English Standard Version®), © 2001 by Crossway, a publishing ministry of Good News Publishers. | Scripture quotations marked (NLT) are taken from the Holy Bible, New Living Translation, copyright ©1996, 2004, 2015 by Tyndale House Foundation. Used by permission of Tyndale House Publishers, Carol Stream, Illinois 60188. All rights reserved. | Scripture taken from the New King James Version®. Copyright © 1982 by Thomas Nelson. Used by permission. All rights reserved.

ISBN:

Ronnie D. Simmons

"Pleasant words are as a honeycomb, sweet to the soul and health to the bones."

(Proverbs 16:24 KJV)

"And I went unto the angel, and said unto him, Give me the little book. And he said unto me, take it, and eat it up; and it shall make thy belly bitter, but it shall be in thy mouth sweet as honey."

(Revelation 10:9 KJV)

"Words are like bees; some create honey and others leave a sting."

(Author-Unknown)

"He is not worthy of the honeycomb, that shuns the hives, because the bees have sting."

(William Shakespeare)

"Anyone who thinks they're too small to make a difference has never met the honeybee."

(Pastor Ronnie D. Simmons)

DEDICATION

*T*his is the first book I have ever written, and at age 66, I am very grateful for God's amazing favor and patience. I dedicate this book to the love, labor, life, and legacy of my parents, Ernest F. and Mattie M. Simmons. Throughout their lives, they laid a strong foundation for me, teaching and demonstrating a diligent work ethic while showing compassion and concern for others. Although they have both transitioned from their **"earthly houses to a building from God, a house not made with hands, eternal in the heavens;"** their legacy still lives on.

My mother often quoted Psalm 106:1, **"Praise the Lord! Oh, give thanks to the Lord; for He is good! For His mercy endures forever."** My father often quoted Proverbs 3:5-6, **"Trust in the Lord with all your heart, and lean not on your own understanding: In all your ways acknowledge Him, And He shall direct your paths."** Through these teachings of my parents, I learned to exhibit both an "attitude of gratitude" and an unwavering faith and confidence in the Lord. To both Mr. Ernest and Mrs. Mattie Simmons, I say: "Thank you" and I look forward to seeing you again in our new heavenly home.

Ronnie D. Simmons

ACKNOWLEDGMENTS

I am so grateful to my Heavenly Father for allowing me to minister in the Gospel Ministry to His precious people for more than 40 years. I am indebted to three spiritual fathers who have birthed, mentored, trained, disciplined and loved me despite my shortcomings. The late Rev. Dr. Enoch Jones, pastor of the historic Fifteenth Avenue Missionary Baptist Church in Nashville, Tennessee, was my first spiritual father. He mentored me through my early training as a gospel preacher. Next, I received the baptism of the Holy Ghost from my second spiritual father, Pastor Bill McRay of Victory Fellowship Church and Victory Bible Training Center, also in Nashville. He instructed me in the development of my faith. Finally, my current spiritual father, Dr. Creflo A. Dollar of World Changers Church International in College Park, Georgia, taught me how to "Dream Big" and how to be a spiritual son and a spiritual father.

Ronnie D. Simmons

    I am especially grateful to the disciples of the House of Faith Christian Center in Smyrna, Tennessee for their encouragement, prayers, and support as they follow my leadership to "Exalt the Savior, Equip the Saints, and Evangelize the Sinner." You are truly a "Compassion in Action" Ministry church.

    I am grateful to my siblings: Marilyn, Barbara, and Michael (Christine) who are all involved in ministry in the Kingdom of God, and who continue to carry out the legacy of our parents. Thank you, Ms. Tonya Jones, Dr. Tamara Henry, Ms. Charisse Henry, and Dr. Kaye Jeter, for guiding me through the publishing process, editing this manuscript, and for challenging me to think and write from a reader's perspective.

    To my Covenant brother from a "different mother"; Dr. Alexander Arthur for your wise counsel, and inspiration, and for assisting me in publishing this book.

    Finally, I am grateful to my bride of more than 44 years, Pastor Terrie R. Simmons. Thank you for your patience, support, and prayers. To the entire Simmons "tribe", including my son Joshua and daughter-in-love Sierra, daughter Jessica Rouse and son-in-love Vince, and all my grandchildren: Essence, Exavier, Kaleb, Kannon, Shiloh, and our bonus child, Levi. You are all a blessing to me.

    To you all, I say continue to Love one another as Jesus has loved you and continue to show "Compassion in Your Actions." Pastor Ronnie D. Simmons

Table of Contents

Dedication iv
Acknowledgments... vi
The 3 b's that do not sting... 1
Introduction 2

PART 1

Chapter 1: Bees That Do Sting ……………....…..11

Chapter 2: Section 1. Bees in the Bible 22

Chapter 3: Section 2. Bees in the Bible ……..……... 29

PART 2

The Three-Step Process to Christian Discipleship

Chapter 4: Step 1. Be-Coming a Be-liever 38

Chapter 5: Step 2. Be-Coming A Be-Longer 53

Chapter 6: Step 3. Be-ing A Be-Comer..................... 68

PART 3

Chapter 7: Summary 80

Chapter 8: Resources 85

About The Author 98

Ronnie D. Simmons

Considering the Bees

The 3 B's That Do Not Sting

The Three-Step Process to Christian Discipleship

Introduction

As I began to understand the importance in my Christian life to being strong in the Lord, I thought in terms of there being different parts of growing. You see, if you miss one, you could be stung, just like being stung by a bee. I am sure you will agree with me that nobody, I mean nobody likes to be stung by anything. People have died from being stung and missed having this wonderful gift of eternal life.

About the Bees

As a resident of planet Earth for more than 66 years, I have been fascinated with one of God's most mysterious insects, Bees. I am told that there are an estimated 20,000 species of the 2 billion bees that inhabit the earth. However, I am only familiar with three types of Bees: the honeybee, the bumble bee, and the killer bee.

The honeybee is known for making sweet honey; it is domesticated and can live up to three years. The bumble bee is known for its loud humming sound, it does not like to be disturbed and can live up to one year. Finally, Killer bees fly in large swarms and are easily agitated when disturbed.

What is common among all three types of these bees is their ability to sting, which is very painful - and sometimes deadly - to people and animals alike. Only the female bee can puncture the skin and embed the stinger in the victim in such a way that it cannot be pulled out without tearing loose from the bee's abdomen and injecting acidic venom. Statistics show an average of 53 deaths from bee stings are reported each year.

So, what do you do when a Bee appears before you? I know you do what I would do, you will try to swat at it, and then you would move away really fast!

This is the reason why many people have phobias about bees, and for good reason. The sting hurts. The severity of the pain of the sting is based on four conditions:

1. Where on the body has the bee stung you?
2. How many times has the bee stung you?
3. What is the size or length of the stinger in your body?

4. How long does the stinger stay in your body before it is removed?

Bees Do Sting

In a spiritual sense, as it relates to the pain of a sting; the Apostle Paul; who wrote half of the New Testament, states these challenging words; **"O death where is thy sting? O grave where is thy victory? The sting of death is sin, and the power of sin is the law"** 1 Corinthians 15:55-56 KJV.

In this book "3 B's That Do Not Sting," I divide the book into three parts. In Part 1, Chapters 1-3, I share vital information about Bees, Bees in the Bible, and the Bee's Sting analogy to capture your attention. I will compare the pain and hurt of the bee's sting to the pain and hurt of the effects of sin in our lives. In addition, just as there are some practical ways how to avoid being stung by a bee. I reveal some insightful and inspiring ways you can avoid being stung by the harmful effects of sin. In the Book of Proverbs, King Solomon advises us to **go to the Ant, consider her ways, and be wise** (Proverbs 6:6 KJV). Today, I stand amazed at how we can also go to the Bee and consider its ways and find teachable principles to avoid being stung not only by the Bee but also by sin.

Finally, I conclude by uncovering the interesting observations of how bees, on one hand, will sting you, however, on the other hand, they are consistent and diligent when they come together for a common purpose. Just as King Solomon instructs us to go to the ant, consider her ways, and be wise; I will share with you 10 biblical lessons you can learn from the ways of the Bee while you are serving God, and progressing on your spiritual journey as a citizen in the Kingdom of God. Just like you consider the ways of the ant, when you consider the ways of the bee, you will become wise.

In Part 2, Chapters 4-6, I express in the spiritual sense, there are three (3) Bees that do not sting, nor will they ever harm you. Instead, they will wrap you like a cocoon as God's love, and swarm and inject you with his peace, mercy, and grace. There are three words beginning with the letter "B" that I have found very compelling. They are:

1. **Becoming a Be-liever**
2. **Becoming a Be-longer**
3. **Being a Be-comer**

In these chapters, I will introduce to you my personal side of the three steps of becoming a Be-liever; becoming a be-longer; and being a be-comer. Next, I will discuss what God has revealed to me about it. Finally, I will offer an opportunity to affirm this information in your life. Affirmations are to be read aloud so that they become a part of your daily living.

Ronnie D. Simmons

My Personal Experience

My Friend, you may be thinking, "Is all of this necessary?" Allow me to share something with you from a personal experience. I have been a pastor of the Church of the Lord Jesus Christ since 1984. I have encountered, counseled, advised, and prayed for hundreds of "church folk." What I discovered is that the most effective and efficient Christians are those who openly and verbally confess the Lord Jesus and show through actions and changed behavior that they believe the Bible. We get to God through his Son Jesus, who came to Earth to first demonstrate a Christian lifestyle and then allow himself to be falsely accused so he could die on the cross for our sins and rise again to give us hope of eternal life.

At this point in our walk, we know without a doubt that God loves us. Getting to the first B, Be-liever, is fantastic. But to grow and develop as a Christian, we need the second B, Be-**longer.**

If you ever thought you were a loner or alone, then it's essential that you become a be-longer. The world says we should seek to belong to Girl and Boy Scouts as a child, to Little League and dance classes as a youth, to Student Government as a high school student, to a sorority or fraternity in higher education, to the fitness center around the corner as a young adult, to the PTA as a parent and to the Rotary, Lion's Club or Masons as a mature adult. In other words, we should strive to be an accepted part of the crowd. The Bible, however, focuses on belonging to a different crowd, the Family of God.

Once we have established God's love as a Be-liever, we show the world we are a Be-longer when we follow the New Commandment of Jesus in John 13:34-35, which tells us "**A new commandment I give unto you, that you also love one another as I have loved you, that you love one another. By this all will know that you are my disciples if you have love for one another**" NKJV. Then again, Romans 14:8 ESV tells us, "**For if we live, we live to the Lord, and if we die, we die to the Lord. So then, whether we live or whether we die, we are the Lord's.**"

Being a **Be-liever** and a **Be-longer** is not complete until that final step of being a **Be-comer** is taken place. Have you ever wanted to follow in the footsteps of someone so badly – say become "just like them" – that you carefully study their mannerisms, their speech patterns, the things they like or dislike? This is how believers should be in their relationship with Jesus. You seek to be a **Be-comer**.

All three of these positions are required if a person desires to be all that God wants them to be, and for them to fulfill their purpose and destiny in life. The entire process can be compared to a competitive race; but not a quick 100 or 200-meter sprint. It's like training for the Olympics. Olympic athletes often start training in their childhood and commit to a full training schedule after embracing the fact that they'll have to make major life changes to be able to compete on an elite level.

Christians must go through a similar process, committing to the three B's as they accept God's offer of a New Life that requires an obedient lifestyle. The Christian race will require endurance, patience, and faith to complete it, much like the life of an athlete. In fact, the Hebrew writer says it this way: **"Since we are surrounded by a great cloud of witnesses, let us run with endurance the race that is set before us, looking unto Jesus, the founder and perfecter of our faith"** Hebrews 12:1-2 ESV.

The Origin of the Book Title

I would like to share with you how I came up with the title, **"Three B's That Do Not Sting."**

The year was 1977, and I had just returned from attending a Youth Retreat in Houston Texas, where for the first time, I had asked Jesus Christ to be both my Lord and Savior. I was on "fire for the Lord." Because of this passion, I was asked by my pastor to begin a new ministry at our church called; The "Baptist Training Union" (B.T.U). As a Christian Leader, my motto was "Train well, to Serve well". In my study preparations, I came across some Christian materials entitled, *"B's that Never Sting."* I began to share these informative and inspirational teachings with my class.

Ten years later, in 1987, as a pastor, I purchased a set of New Testament paperback commentaries by author Warren Wiersbe entitled; *The Be Series: The Book of Acts through The Book of Revelation.* I began to preach and teach our church congregation from these dynamic commentaries. Through these two spiritual experiences, the seed for the book; **"Three B's That Do Not Sting"**; was planted.

As a pastor of a thriving and energetic nondenominational church, I am a proponent of "spiritual pediatrics" which is Christian Discipleship. Our church promotes a three-fold vision of Exalting the Savior; Equipping the Saints; and Evangelizing the Sinner. We have Five Purposes which are: Evangelism, Worship, Fellowship, Discipleship, and Ministry. In addition, I believe that Disciples are made not born.

My Purpose for Writing this Book:

The purpose of this book is to introduce you to the three steps of Be-ing a follower of Jesus Christ, based upon the Word of God, that are expected and vital for Christian Discipleship. As you read each page of this book, I believe that you will study and meditate on it for your own spiritual enrichment and edification.

In addition, you will receive important INFORMATION that will lead to an eye-opening REVELATION, which will eventually lead to a total mind-boggling TRANSFORMATION of your life. And so, in keeping with the instructions of Jesus before He departed, where He admonished us to **"Go therefore and make disciples of all the nations, baptizing them in the name of the Father, and of the**

son and of the Holy Spirit, teaching them to observe all things that I have commanded you; and lo, I am with you always, even to the end of the age...," Matt. 28:18-20 (NKJV), I pen this book.

Enjoy and Be Blessed in Jesus!

Pastor Ronnie D. Simmons

PART 1

Chapter 1

Bees That Do Sting

M y friend, have you ever been stung by a Bee or have you heard what it feels like? Well, getting stung by a bee is something no one could ever want to experience. Here are some of the effects. It is painful. It hurts and causes swelling, itching, and other allergic reactions.

In this chapter, I want to address two inquisitive questions:

1) Why do Bees sting?
2) How do I avoid being stung by a Bee?

However, before addressing these two questions, I would like to share a couple of stories of individuals who had some unpleasant incidences with unfriendly Bees.

Jack shares his personal story about an encounter with a swarm of Bees:

"I went to Kiva Elementary School in Scottsdale, Arizona. It was in the late 1950s or early 1960s. I was in the 6th grade and my younger sister was in the 5th grade. It was the last class of the day, which was my Physical Education class and we along with our classmates were playing on the playground outside. All of a sudden, and out of nowhere, a swarm of Bees, came swooping down. I then yelled as loud as I could, 'Hit the deck'! Fortunately, these bees were heading across to an orange grove located on the other side of the playground. Otherwise, all of us would have been stung that day."

Dee gave his encounter with a certain Bee and relates it to spiritual insights:

"While walking in the field one day with my two young sons, a Bee from one of my hives made a beeline for my elder son and stung him above his right eye. He quickly brushed it away and threw himself in the grass, kicking, and screaming for help. The Bee then went straight for my younger son and began buzzing around his head. The next thing I knew, he too was lying in the grass, yelling at the top of his lungs. But I picked him up and told him to stop crying and assured him by saying; 'That Bee is harmless and it cannot hurt you, because it has lost its sting."

Ronnie D. Simmons

I took that frightened young boy over to his older brother, showed him the little black stinger in his brow and said; 'The bee can buzz around and scare you, but it is powerless to hurt you because your older brother took the sting away by being stung.'

I then explained to him, 1 Corinthians 15:56, which tells us the sting of death is sin, but our elder brother, the Lord Jesus hung on the cross and took the sting out of death by dying in our place. Since the law demands satisfaction only once, death is powerless to hurt us if we accept the work of Jesus Christ on the cross on our behalf. The unbeliever is filled with fear because he must face God with his sin. But for us, death's sting is gone, because it was left in Jesus. Death may still buzz around and attempt to scare us at times, but it can no longer have us."

Question #1: Why Do Bees Sting?

Most stinging situations occur between humans and stinging insects like the Bee, because of two situations.

1. The Bee feels threatened and it is its nature to sting
2. You are too close to the hive

One famous author shares her experience in her childhood, running barefooted through the summer clove. This resulted in honeybee stings on numerous occasions. She states that a sting in your bare foot really hurts. Full of frustration, she thought to herself; "why did this Bee sting me? I did not do anything wrong from my point of view. Actually, I did do harm to the Bee, although I did not mean to hurt it."

Secondly, it is the nature of the bee to sting. Just as it is the nature of a cow to moo; the nature of a dog to bark; and the nature of a bird to chirp; it is the nature of a bee to sting.

Bee stings are usually a form of defense. Bees are defending themselves because they feel threatened. In addition, a sting is an effort to drive you away from their nest.

The Worker Bees guard the area near the nest, inside is the next generation of baby bees; and food for the colony is critical if the hive is to survive.

From a spiritual perspective, the word "sting" is a reference to sin. Sin affects all of us in basically two ways:

1. Sin affects our society and nation. All of us are witnesses to an increase in homicides and suicides, abortions, thefts, bodily harm, child abuse, arson, sexual sins, etc. These are what I refer to as "Sins in the Streets." However, there is also an increase in embezzlement, tax fraud, treason, perjury, cyberattacks, etc. These are what I refer to as "Sins in the Sweets."

As these sins of "Sins in the Streets" and "Sins in the Sweets" continue to increase and plague our nation, the fabric of ethics, morality, and righteousness will continue to unravel us from the seam. Notice what the psalmist says in Psalm 14:34, **"righteousness exalteth a nation, but sin is a reproach to any people."**

2. In addition to our society and nation, sin attempts to affect our spirit, our soul, and our body. The Apostle Paul says in Romans 6:23 these insightful words; **"For the wages of sin is death ..."** There is the penalty of sin, the power of sin, and the presence of sin. But Praise be unto God, for we now have the answer to the sin problem in our nation, our spirit, our soul, and in our body.

His name is Jesus Christ, the Son of the Living God. Matthew 1:21 states; **"And his name shall be called Jesus, for he shall save His people from their sins."** Because of Jesus dying on the cross for our sins, when we accept Him as our Lord and Savior, we are now saved and delivered from the Penalty of sin, in our spirit. When we follow the teachings of Jesus and are led by the Holy Spirit, then we are saved and delivered from the Power of sin in our souls.

When we present our body as a holy, dedicated, and living sacrifice unto the Lord, we are saved and delivered from the presence of sins in our body.

The 3 B's That Do Not Sting

> *"O Death, where is your sting? O grave, where is your victory? The sting of death is sin, and the power of sin is the law. But thanks be to God who gives us the victory through our Lord Jesus Christ"* 1 Corinthians 15:55-57

Question #2: How Do I Avoid Being Stung By A Bee?

There are basically two ways you can avoid being stung by a bee.
1. Keep your distance from a bee colony, nest, or hive, and/or
2. Wear protective clothing

The easiest and most effective way of avoiding stings is to keep your distance from a nest, colony, or swarm. However, if you happen to stumble upon one, walk swiftly and calmly in the opposite direction. This will prevent you from further riling the nest of bees. You should also make your exit in a straight line, as running zigzag will keep you in the danger zone longer. It is also good to note that if a swarm of bees attacks you, run as fast as you can away from it and preferably toward people who may be able to assist you. By removing yourself from the immediate vicinity, you may be able to prove to the bees that you are not a threat and they are more likely to leave you alone.

However, if you are dealing with one or two bees buzzing around your head, don't freak out, chances are the bee is just investigating to assess the threat. If you swat at it, or violently jerk from the situation, you may be indicating that you are in trouble and it is an invitation for the bee to sting you.

Just as you would do your best to avoid and flee from being stung by bees, as Christians we are instructed by the Apostle Paul to Flee from being stung by sin by following these instructions:

- **"FLEE fornication. Every sin that a man doeth is without the body; but he that committeth fornication sinneth against his own body"** 1 Corinthians 6:18 KJV.
- **Wherefore, my dearly beloved, FLEE from idolatry"** 1 Corinthians 10:14 KJV.
- **For the love of money is the root of all evil: which while some have coveted after, they have erred from the faith, and pierced themselves through with many sorrows. But thou, O man of God, FLEE these things; and follow after righteousness, godliness, faith, love, patience, meekness"** 1 Timothy 6:10-11 KJV.

The second way of avoiding stings is to wear protective apparel when you are around bees. This protective garment is referred to as a Beekeeping Suit and it consists of a full body gear, gloves, and a headgear with a mask. This body gear will cover the entire body, from the top of the head to the soles of your feet. Both the gloves and headgear with the mask, when worn properly, will keep the most persistent bees from stinging you. The Beekeeping Suit also must provide proper ventilation for breathing and be flexible enough for you to move around without any restrictions.

Finally, bees are less threat when the beekeeping suit is adorned in all white. For some reason, stained and colored garments seem to irritate the bees which will cause them to release their sting without warning.

In Ephesians 6:11-18, the Apostle instructs us **to resist the wiles, strategies, and schemes of the devil, by taking on the whole armor of God.** This armor consists of seven pieces of garments which are spiritual forces to combat the spiritual wickedness that we are confronted with on a daily basis.

The first three pieces of Spiritual Armor that are worn continually on the battleground, are:

1) The Girdle of Truth

Truth, by its very definition, is exclusive. It means something is true, and other things are lies. Satan is a liar, the father of lies, and every lie finds its origin in him. Every other piece of the full armor of God is attached to the girdle of truth. Jesus said **God's Word is true.** (John 17:17). If you do not begin with the truth, you will never defeat the "sting of sin."

2) The Breastplate of Righteousness

Righteousness means being made right with God. In daily spiritual battles, we need both the complete righteousness of Jesus Christ and the continuing righteousness that comes as a response to God's gift.

Obedience to God protects your heart from the "sting of sin."

3) Shoes of the Gospel of Peace

In Greek, "peace" means oneness or wholeness. The gospel which means good news, is the forgiveness of sins and brings you into oneness with God through faith in the Lord Jesus Christ. This oneness with the Lord produces peace. When we carry anxiousness and worry with us, we are robbed of peace. But the gospel of peace will keep your feet firm and keep you from the "sting of sin." The next three pieces of Spiritual Armor are to be kept ready for use when the actual battle begins.

4) The Shield of Faith

When the Apostle Paul wrote this passage, Roman soldiers carried shields that were covered with heavy animal hide. Before a battle, they would dip their shields into the water so that when the fiery darts hit them, the wet hide would extinguish the darts.

Similarly, a Christian's shield of faith needs to be dipped into the water of God's word to be replenished and fully functional, because **"faith comes by hearing, and hearing by the word of God."** (Romans 10:17) The Shield of Faith will protect you from the "sting of sin."

5) The Helmet of Salvation

The helmet of salvation rests on the work of Jesus Christ to save us, but also involves us as we journey with the Lord and allow Him to work that salvation into every part of our thoughts. The battlefield of the mind is the primary place where spiritual battles are fought. The enemy fights for strongholds to bind us, however, the helmet of salvation will protect us from the "sting of sin."

6) Sword of the Spirit

Word of God. Whenever we are tempted by the lust of the eyes, the lust of the flesh, or the pride of life; the most effective weapon that God has given us as believers is the Sword of the Spirit which is the Word of God. When Jesus was tempted in the wilderness, each time he responded with the truth of God's word. The Sword of the Spirit which is the Word of God will protect you from the "sting of sin."

7) The Garment is Prayer

The prayer life of the believer must be frequent, observant, and persistent, and must line up and be submitted to the will of God. A strong prayer life based on the word of God will protect you from the "sting of sin."

> Additionally, the most effective and efficient beekeeper will always wear white garments; not stained garments. Bees are less agitated and hostile when it comes to the color white.

White garments in the bible refer to holiness and purity. White garments are reserved for:

Jesus
**"Now after six days, Jesus took Peter, James, and John, and led them up on a high mountain apart by themselves; and He was transfigured before them. His clothes became shining, exceedingly WHITE, like snow, such as no
launderer on earth can white them"** Mark 9:2-3 KJV.

The Angels
"Now after the Sabbath, as the first day of the week began to dawn, Mary Magdalene and the other Mary came to see the tomb. And behold, there was a great earthquake; for an angel of the Lord

descended from heaven, and came and rolled back the stone from the door, and sat on it. His countenance was like lightning, and his clothing as WHITE as snow"** Matthew 28:1-3 KJV.

The Redeemed of the Lord
"He who overcomes shall be clothed in WHITE garments, and I will not blot out his name from the Book of Life, but I will confess his name before My Father and before His angels" Revelation 3:5 KJV.

In Conclusion: A Beekeeper who is fully clothed from head to toe in his white beekeeper suit is less likely to be stung by bees. In like manner, a believer who is fully clothed with the whole Armor of God and is clothed in holiness and purity is protected and less likely to be "stung by sin" from the enemy.

Chapter 2

Section 1

Bees In The Bible

*A*nd the Amorites who dwelt in that mountain came out against you and chased you as BEES do, and drove you back from Seir to Hormah." (Deuteronomy 1:44 KJV).

"Then he went down and talked with the woman, and she pleased Samson well. After some time, when he returned to get her, he turned aside to see the carcass of the lion. And behold, a swarm of BEES and honey were in the carcass of the lion." (Judges 14:7-8 KJV).

"They surround me like BEES; They were quenched like a fire of thorns; For in the name of the Lord, I will destroy them." (Psalm 118:12 KJV).

"And it shall come to pass in that day, That the Lord will whistle for the fly That is in the farthest

part of the rivers of Egypt, and for the BEE that is in the land of Assyria" (Isaiah 7:18 KJV).

These scriptures are a reference to the powerful little creatures called Bees. These bees with their harmful and sometimes deadly sting can cause significant pain and were compared in the Old Testament to the power of the enemy nations, like a swarm of bees that attack.

However, from a positive perspective, as Christians, we are encouraged to be more like bees. We are to work united as a team, within the church, the church which is the body of Christ. With tenacity, dedication, commitment, and strength like the bee, we will reap sweet rewards like "honey" from our Lord and be swarmed by His presence, power, and protection.

Biblical Meaning of Bees

Bees in the bible are symbols of productivity, prosperity, hard work, and diligence. They represent abundance, rich, beautiful, and sweet as paradise.

Even the Judge's name "Deborah" in Hebrew means "Bee." Deborah is the name of the prophetess in the Old Testament. She was a poet and the only female judge mentioned in the bible. She led a revolt that helped the Israelites to win their freedom from the Canaanites.

The victory song that she wrote, is found in the Book of Judges today. Listen to these courageous and inspiring words.

"In the days of Shamgar, son Anath, In the days of Jael, the highways were deserted, And the travelers walked along the byways. Village life ceased, it ceased in Israel,[6] Until I Deborah, arose, Arose a mother of Israel. They chose new gods;[7] Then there was war in the gates; Not a shield or spear was seen among forty thousand in Israel. My heart is with the rulers of Israel,[8] Who offered themselves willingly with the people. Bless the Lord.[9] Awake, awake, Deborah![11b] Awake, awake, sing a song![12a] Thus let all your enemies perish, O Lord![30b] But let those who love Him be like the sun, when it comes out in full strength. So, the land had rest for forty years"[31] (Judges 5:6-9, 11b, 12a, 30b, 31 NKJV).

Because of Deborah's tenacity, and her relationship with the God of Abraham, Isaac, and Jacob, she was determined that nobody was going to "sting" her or the Lord's people. Therefore, if you have a little daughter by the name of Deborah, then she can get a buzz out of the history of her name.

10 Lessons We Can Learn from Bees Regarding Serving God

Have you ever thought about the things we could learn from bees? It is not about the honey; on the contrary, it is about Worship and Service. Okay, I know what some of you may be thinking, "Pastor Simmons you may have been stung one too many times". However, if I have stirred up your curiosity just a little bit, here are ten (10) Lessons we can learn from bees about being good Christians. In this Chapter, we will begin our observation with four of them and we will conclude in the next chapter.

#1: Always Be On The Lookout.

Whenever you approach a hive, the first thing you may notice is, the concentration of bees becomes thicker the closer you get to the hive. What you may not have known is that your approach to the hive did not go unnoticed. That is because of the scouts. These are the bees that are always on the lookout for danger.

We need to be able to identify the things that are bad for us. At the same time, we should also be on the lookout for those things that nourish our spirit, soul, and body. Too often, we fall into the trap of spiritual starvation and deny our souls of that which we need for

survival. We are unable to recognize our enemies and then complain about
our situation. However, Jesus Christ has already won the victory over Satan; we have just failed to collect the spoils. Peter admonishes us **to "Be sober, be vigilant because your adversary the devil walks about like a roaring lion, seeking whom he may devour"** (1 Peter 5:8 NKJV).

#2: Get Rid Of Anything That Would Hamper Your Productivity.

Bees keep a clean hive. They remove all foreign matter and debris before beginning the work of storing honey.

Let me ask you a few questions. Are you storing some wasteful clutter in your mind? Do you need to remove some distractions from your life? Are you working to your full potential? What are those things you need from your normal routine to increase your productivity? Several years ago, I preached a dynamic and unforgettable sermon entitled; "It's time to remove the Junk from your Trunk!" Take a lesson from the bees and get rid of anything that is unnecessary in your life.

The author of the book of Hebrews admonishes us **that "since we are compassed about with so great a cloud of witnesses, let us lay aside every weight, and the sin which doth so easily beset us, and let us run** with patience the race that is set before us" (Hebrews 12:1 KJV).

#3: Know When To Cut Certain People Out Of Your Life.

There are three main categories of Bees; Drones, Workers, and Queens. During the winter when food is scarce, the worker bees run the drones out of the hive to preserve food.

Sometimes we have a bad habit of having developed friendships with individuals where the relationship becomes toxic. We pursue these relationships to the point of regressing instead of progressing and they become unhealthy for us, spiritually, mentally, physically, and sometimes financially.

The story is told of a young lady who had a wise and observant mother who worked diligently to keep her daughter away from her closest friend. As my mother used to tell me while I was growing up, "Ronnie, if you hang around dogs long enough, you will start catching their fleas." This mother with her keen and watchful eyes could see that this girl was a bad influence on her daughter. However, the daughter thought that her mother was being overprotective, and could not see it at the time.

It wasn't until much later that the daughter saw and experienced first-hand the negative influence that her friend was having on her. She eventually severed all ties with her.

Are we allowing the closest people in our lives to open our eyes to the negative effects that our friends and acquaintances are having on us? When the apostle Paul cautioned us, **"Do not be unequally yoked together with unbelievers. For what partnership has righteousness with lawlessness, or what fellowship has light with darkness"** (2 Corinthians 6:14 ESV)? He was teaching us to be careful of who we allow to influence our lives.

#4: Know Your Role In The Kingdom.

The queen's job is to mate and lay eggs. The workers feed the queen, harvest pollen, clean the hive, and make honey. Some Bees are nurses, others are scouts, and some lay unfertilized eggs (aka drones). Each bee has a role to play in the hive.

What is your role in the Kingdom of God? Do you know it? Have you taken any steps to find your kingdom's purpose? Have you listened to the still small voice that tries to influence you towards a particular calling? You must know your calling or purpose in life. This is what pushes you to wake up in the morning ready to face the new day. The apostle Paul beseeches us to **walk worthy of that calling which we are called.** (Ephesians 4:1 NKJV).

Review from this chapter

#1-Always be on the lookout
#2-Get rid of anything that would hamper your productivity
#3-Know when to cut certain people out of your life
#4-Know your role in the kingdom

We will continue to address the subject of lessons we can learn from Bees in serving God in the next chapter.

Chapter 3

Section 2

Bees in The Bible

*I*n the previous chapter, Section 1; we discovered that bees in the bible are symbols of productivity, prosperity, hard work, and diligence. They also represent abundance.

In addition, we are encouraged to be more like bees, and work united as a team, with the church, which is the body of Christ. Finally, we stated that with tenacity, dedication, commitment, and strength like the bee, we will reap sweet rewards like "honey" from our Lord.

We concluded the chapter by examining lessons we can learn from bees regarding serving God.

They are:

#1-Always be on the lookout
#2-Get rid of anything that would hamper your productivity
#3-Know when to cut people out of your life.
#4-Know your role in the kingdom

We will continue with lessons 5-10 in this chapter.

#5: Give Your Allegiance To One Ruler.

There can only be one queen in a hive. In cases where there are two queens in one hive, the second queen has to either leave the hive or be killed.

We each have what I call a "god-slot." We are either going to fill it with Jehovah, or we are going to fill it with an idol. Idolatry is not all golden calves and passing our children through the fire which was exhibited in the Old Testament.

It can be as simple as overeating, gossiping, worrying, jealousy, and envy. It could even be social media. We were meant to serve one ruler and that is what we should do.

"And if it seems evil to you to serve the Lord, choose for yourselves this day whom you will serve....

But as for me and my house, we will serve the Lord" (Joshua 24:15 NKJV).

#6: The Sovereign Receives Only The Best.

Drones eat pollen and honey. Queens eat royal jelly. I must admit that the first time I heard this, I laughed. I asked myself, is it only the queen who eats royal jelly?

However, let's extract this lesson from the bee and apply it to worship. If we gave God the best of what we have; our time, our efforts, our words, our worship, our praise; what would it look like? What would it sound like? Would it be worthy of a king? Would it be royal jelly? The Apostle Paul says, **"For we are to God the fragrance of Christ among those who are being saved and among those who are perishing...the aroma of life leading to life."** (2 Corinthians 2: 15-16 NKJV). At the same time according to the prophet Isaiah, **"If you are willing and obedient, you shall eat the good of the land."** (Isaiah 1:19 NKJV).

#7: They Live To Serve.

Baby bees feed the queen. Worker bees store the pollen and make honey. Scouts are on the lookout for food and danger. The drones give their lives to mate with the queen.

How are we serving the master? One of the reasons why God wants us to be made free from sin is that we can serve him in spirit and in truth. The Apostle Paul understood it clearly when he said, **"Being then made free from sin, ye became servants of righteousness."** (Romans 6: 18 NKJV). This statement attests to the fact that we should be more concerned about how we live our lives, not just what we achieve or who we are to the world. God is more concerned about our character than our pedigree, our actions more than our words, and our service more than our status.

#8: Bees Are Ready To Give Their Lives For A Cause.

If I ask the question, "What would you die for? What would be your answer?" I'll be totally honest; I don't know what my answer will be. But I want it to be Jesus, don't you? I want to be willing like the apostles to die for him.

Why? Because my life is in His hand and I am nothing without Him. Why? Like the apostle Paul, I am **"confident, I say, and willing rather to be absent**

from the body, and to be present with the Lord. Wherefore we labor, that whether present or absent, we may be accepted of Him." (2 Corinthians 5: 8-9 KJV).

Bees routinely give their lives to defend the hive. Would you give your life to defend other believers? As true believers who have given our lives over to Jesus, we must ponder on the question before we answer, even as we are reminded of Jesus' words when He said, **"For whoever desires to save his life will lose it, but whoever loses his life for My sake will find it."** (Matthew 16:25 NKJV).

#9: Work For The Common Good.

Bees have a number of predators. In a weak hive, the predators thrive. Dozens of bees are eaten by lizards and birds. Beetles, moths, ants, and roaches invade the hives and make it unpalatable for the bees. At that point, the bees are very dependent on the beekeeper to tend the hive and rid it of these intruders. If too many of these enemies invade the hive, the bees will leave.

But when the hives are strong, the bees defend themselves. They will attack anything that doesn't belong. Together, they are strong enough to kill a lizard. I have even heard stories of bees stinging cows to death. One bee is just a little sting, but a hive of bees? They are a lethal weapon. Now this is a unique lesson we can learn from the bees.

As Christians, when we pull our strengths, talents, abilities, and resources together, we will become so powerful that no weapon the enemy brings against us, will defeat us. This was made evident, in the 1950s and 1960s, when Black Americans led by a Gospel Preacher by the name of Dr. Martin L. King Jr. joined forces together in the name of a common cause called Civil rights and defeated in a large part of the enemies of segregation, injustice, and Jim Crow laws.

As I reflect back on the impact of the Civil Rights movement and how this Non-violent charismatic leader was able to unite all people from diverse backgrounds; Blacks and Whites, Jews and Gentiles, Protestants and Catholics, males and females. I am reminded of a future event that involves a similar unification of diverse people. Unlike the Civil Rights movement, this event will take place not on earth, but in heaven. Listen to John the Revelator,

"After these things, I looked, and behold, a great multitude which no one could number, of all nations, tribes, peoples, and tongues standing before the throne and before the Lamb, clothed with white robes, with branches in their hands and crying out with a loud voice, saying, 'Salvation belongs to our God who sits on the throne, and to the Lamb" (Revelation 7:9-10).

Ronnie D. Simmons

#10: Teamwork Produces Golden Treasures.

In Samson's day, the men of the city in their attempt to discover the source of his strength, asked him, **"What's sweeter than honey'?"** (Judges 14:18 NKJV). Thousands of years and many experiences later, the answer would still be the same. Nothing!

Now I hope I don't gross you out by telling you that the delicious honey you enjoyed on your biscuits or toast this morning for breakfast is a result of dozens of bees vomiting into each other's mouths. Yes, this is the beautiful result of hours of bee labor and hundreds of miles flown to get the perfect blend of nectar and pollen that we all enjoy daily.

What beautiful treasures would God's children be able to create if they worked together in love? The possibilities are almost endless when one contemplates the power of our creative God.

Allow me to share with you a testimony of how teamwork can produce golden treasures when people love each other and trust God. In 1984, I was called to pastor a church in Murfreesboro Tennessee (30 miles southeast of Nashville) which had only existed for less than a few months. The congregation was small; we had little money, and we were meeting in the auditorium of a high school. In the summer, we sweated because they forgot to turn on the central air conditioner, and in the wintertime, we were cold, because they forgot to turn on the gas for heating.

This occurred for three years until a miracle took place. Our small congregation was blessed to receive a gift of 2.7 acres of land. We only paid back taxes on the land and the transfer of the deed into the church's name. This cost us less than $1,000.00. We then hired a contractor to build a church facility on our land.

At first, everything was fine. We were still meeting inside the school's auditorium, and the congregation was growing and excited. I expected us to move into our new church building in the Spring of 1988. However, after completing 75% of the project, the contractor ceased working on the church building and eventually sued the church for failing to agree with the terms of the contract. In addition, he placed a lien on the building, which meant that we could not hire another contractor to complete the church building.

When everything was looking bleak and gloomy, we received a blessing from the Lord. A gentleman raised in Murfreesboro as a child returned to the area after retiring from the military. While in the military, he learned how to perform construction work. He united with the church and agreed to complete the construction of the church, free. A licensed plumber and licensed electrician assisted him. The members began to not only assist this precious brother in his work, but they even put me to work, caulking the walls. They used their credit cards and lines of credit to purchase the materials to complete the project. In the Fall of 1988, after much prayer, and favor from the Lord, we marched into our new church facility.

However, the saga did not end when the church opened. Although our church building was finished, the original contractor demanded his money and after we refused to pay him, he took us to court. Our funds were depleted, and we had no attorney to represent us.

Again, the blessing of the Lord showed up. My sister, who was a practicing attorney in Nashville, heard of our predicament and agreed to represent us free. After many court proceedings, the judge finally dismissed the lawsuit and removed the lien placed on our church building. Hallelujah!!

Like bees, we swarmed together as a church congregation in fellowship during tough and trying times, and we experienced the sweet and golden treasure of God's love and favor. It all reminded me of the prophet Nehemiah and the people of Israel, who after much opposition from the enemies who were against the rebuilding of the wall of Jerusalem, prevailed and succeeded, eventually testified, **"So we built the wall, and the entire wall was joined together up to half its height, for the people had a mind to work"** (Nehemiah 4:6 NKJV).

In conclusion, some people may look at bees as simple insects, yet there are so many lessons we can learn from observing Bees. Now let me ask, out of the ten lessons, what was your favorite lesson?

PART 2

The Three-step Process to Christian Discipleship

Chapter 4

Step 1: Be-Coming A Be-Liever

*H*aving considered the Bee, I would like to explore a three-step process that will allow us to discover, understand, and apply the dynamic principles of Christian Discipleship.

The three-step process can be classified as:

Step 1. Becoming a Be-liever
Step 2. Becoming a Be-longer
Step 3. Being a Be-comer

Step 1. Becoming a Be-Liever

The 3 B's That Do Not Sting

My journey to becoming a Be-liever began at age 10. I grew up in a large low-to-middle-class family in Nashville, Tennessee.

We had two wonderful and loving parents and I was the youngest of five siblings. I attended Metro Davidson County Schools where I was an excellent student, and my favorite subjects were mathematics, social studies, and spelling. I rarely got into trouble. They taught me to honor and respect my parents and my elders. My mother was a committed and dedicated homemaker, and my father was an excellent full-time chef at an exquisite private country club in Belle Meade, Tennessee.

Because both of my parents enjoyed cooking, every Sunday after church we had invited (and sometimes uninvited) guests who came by for a delicious meal. The meal would usually be two sizzling meats, several seasoned vegetables, oven-baked cornbread, and desserts such as cake, pies, or cobblers with ice cream.

During Thanksgiving and Christmas, our house was jammed packed, because our relatives knew where to come to receive not only a delicious mouth-watering meal, but laughter, fun, and great fellowship. Yes, it was at the Simmons home.

In addition, I grew up having strong spiritual and religious roots because my maternal grandfather, the Rev. Walter Robert Murray, pastored the well-known

15th Avenue Baptist Church in Nashville for over 25 years. Yes, my mother was a PK (preacher's kid). I would often see her reading the Bible at night and hear her singing church and spiritual songs. My father grew up in Adairsville, Kentucky near the Tennessee line in a family that required church attendance and prohibited alcohol consumption.

With my parents' upbringing, they taught us to pray before our meals. As a family, we would gather around the dinner table and either my mother or father would say "grace." Their favorite bible verse was "Oh give thanks to the Lord, for He is good, and his mercy endures forever." Also, it was expected and required that our family attend Sunday School and church service every Sunday. We attended my "grandfather's church," although my grandfather had died in 1953.

In 1967, when I was an energetic, inquisitive 10-year-old boy, sitting in a church pew one Sunday morning, the pastor concluded his sermon with an invitation to become a member, which we call "Christian Discipleship."

"The doors of the church are now open," the pastor solemnly intoned. Without hesitation, I jumped from the pew, rushed down the aisle, sat in the chair provided by the deacons, and said enthusiastically with a magnificent smile, "I want to be a member of this church, and I want to be baptized."

The feelings I had on that day were greater than any experience I had ever felt. Most of the time, a 10-year-old boy would think about basketball, football, M&M candy, the next Batman episode, or a delicious, homemade dinner after church. None of this crossed my mind that day. A few weeks later, I was baptized and began diligently working in the church.

My evolution was typical. I faithfully attended Sunday School and worship services. A few years later, I joined the church choir, served on the Junior Deacon Board, and became a Junior Usher. At various times, I collected and counted the Sunday morning offerings.

As a teenager, they even gave me a key to the church. As I grew older, I attended revivals, conferences, and retreats. I thought, that I was a believer. But I was mistaken.

Fast forward to 1977, almost exactly 10 years from the time I initially joined the church as a 10-year-old. I was attending a youth conference in Houston, Texas, and met a youth who quickly became a close friend. He asked me two thought-provoking questions:

1. **"If you were to die tonight**, are you 100% sure that you would go to heaven?"

2. **"If you arrived at heaven's door**, and the Lord asked you, 'Why should I allow you to enter,' what would you say?"

My response to the first question was, "I am not sure, but I hope so."

With the second question, I began a long explanation, telling my new friend, "I am a good person. I go to church, and I believe in God."

At that moment, my friend began to share with me the ABCs of Salvation from the Word of God. As a 20-year-old man, this was the very first time I had ever been asked these thought-provoking, mind-boggling questions.

And so, I would like to share with you the first step to Christian Discipleship. The first B that never stings is "Becoming a Be-liever."

The Abc To Salvation: Three Steps

Step A

Admit that you are a sinner and that you deserve to die for your sins.

In the book of Romans, the apostle Paul tells us clearly, **"All have sinned and come short of the glory of God"** (Romans 3:23 NKJV), and, **"The wages of sin is death...."** (Romans 6:23 NKJV). It is very important for all of us to remember that we have done some wrong things in our lives, in some shape or form.

> *You are a sinner, not because you sin, but you sin, because you are a sinner*

The 3 B's That Do Not Sting

Simply put, being a sinner, which is a noun defines who you are. Sinning, which is a verb, defines what you do. We should always remember that what we do should never define who we are. As individuals, we are born into a world of sin. We are shaped into iniquity (Psalms 51:5), and we take on the nature of Adam who was the first man of creation. Think about it, you do not have to teach a child how to lie, steal, or cheat. Because of Adam's sin and disobedience, this nature of his has been passed on to every human being.

I would like for you to consider this: You can take a pig from the mud, clean, shave, thoroughly wash him, dress him, and put shoes on him to change him. However, it will not be long until you will find that same pig, undressed and back in the mud! Why? Because this is his nature. All of us are born with this "sin" nature.

No amount of outward washing and changing of our environment will turn us into a new person. It will take a heart transplant to transform our sinful nature into a new person. 2 Corinthians 5:17 tells **us "Therefore if any man be in Christ, he is a new creature: old things are passed away; behold, all things are become new."**

Step B

Believe that Jesus Christ died on the cross for you and now you are willing to repent of all your sins. Romans 5:8, tells **us "But God commended His own**

love toward us, in that while we were yet sinners, Christ died for us."

Jesus died on the cross, not only to forgive us of our sins but to release us from the power and penalty of our sins. This goodness of God should lead us to repentance, which means we are willing to change our minds and will. This change leads us in a new direction. A direction of belonging to Christ, to the body of Christ, and to the Kingdom of God. Unlike the pig, you are not washed with soap and water, but rather with the blood of Jesus and is now changed from within having not only a new mind of Christ but the power of Christ within you to live Christlike.

It is important to make sure that we do not **"despise the riches of His goodness, forbearance, and longsuffering, not knowing that the goodness of God leads to repentance"** Romans 2:4. It is this repentance that ignites our Christlike nature and faith.

Many people believe that God is angry and upset with them, and the only way for Him to lead people to change and repent is for Him to dispense his wrath upon them. They view God as some mean old man up in heaven, carrying around with Him a 2x4, waiting for every opportunity to whack them upside the head. However, when they see a compassionate, gracious, and good God, then they will come to repent of their sins.

Scriptures For Consideration:

- Ezekiel 11: 19-20
  ¹⁹And I will give them one heart, and I will put a new spirit within you, and I will take the stony heart out of their flesh, and will give them a heart of flesh:

  ²⁰That they may walk in my statutes, and keep mine ordinances, and do them: and they shall be my people, and I will be their God.

- 2 Corinthians 5: 17-18
  ¹⁷Therefore if any man be in Christ, he is a new creature: old things are passed away; behold, all things are become new.

  ¹⁸And all things are of God, who hath reconciled us to himself by Jesus Christ, and hath given to us the ministry of reconciliation;

- Ephesians 4: 22-24
  ²²That ye put off concerning the former conversation the old man, which is corrupt according to the deceitful lusts;

  ²³ And be renewed in the spirit of your mind;

  ²⁴And that ye put on the new man, which after God is created in righteousness and true holiness.

Step C

Confess Jesus as your Lord. First, you need to explain what Be-comer means. Be-comer of what or who. Set the stage for the texts that confirm your definition of a Be-comer.

The apostle Paul admonishes us, **"That if you confess with your mouth the Lord Jesus and believe in your heart that God has raised Jesus from the dead, you will be saved. For with the heart, one believes unto righteousness, and with the mouth, confession is made unto salvation"** (Romans 10:9-10 NKJV).

This begins a new life in Jesus. Take notice of what 2 Corinthians 5:17 says. **"Therefore, if anyone is in Christ, he is a new creation; old things have passed away; behold all things have become new."**

These are the ABCs in becoming a Be-Liever

I mistakenly thought I was a believer after I joined the church. I thought that the way to please God was to be a 'good person' and work in the church. Through my ignorance, I was working in the church to become saved hoping when I died, I would have tallied enough good works or brownie points in the church and in my life, and that my good works would outweigh my bad works. I wanted to hear my Heavenly Father say, "Well done you good and faithful servant."

The 3 B's That Do Not Sting

It was never explained to me that going to church, being baptized through immersion into water, taking communion, and trying to be "a good person" were not the requirements for salvation. The Bible tells us that the Father wants us to accept, acknowledge, and confess His Son Jesus Christ as His perfect gift for our sin problem. Jesus Christ paid my debt, something that He did not owe. I owed a debt that I could not pay.

When talking to people about eternal salvation, the response is often, "I believe in God." I usually tell them that "believing in God" is not sufficient for salvation. Jesus says in His word that to believe in God the Father is to believe also in Me.

In the book of John, He said **"Let not your heart be troubled: ye believe in God, believe also in me,"** (John 14:1 NKJV). Jesus then continues to explain in this chapter of John that **"He is the way, He is the truth, and He is the life. No man can come to the Father (God), unless they come by Him"** (Jesus) (John 14:6 NKJV). This means that Jesus Christ is the only way and the only one who can reconcile and connect a Holy and Righteous God to Unrighteous Sinners Like us.

Belief in God has trended downward since the early 2000s. A recent Gallup Poll found a majority will answer positively if asked the simple question, "Do you believe in God?" The certainty of knowing God decreases if people are given the option to answer with more than a simple "yes" or "no." For example, adults were not as certain if asked if they are convinced God exists with 64% of U.S. adults expressing certainty about the existence of God; but a quarter of those asked said God "probably exists but they have doubts and 6% said God probably doesn't exist and 7% were convinced God doesn't exist.

As a teen, I knew God existed because I believed Jesus Christ was a real person. Jesus existed, walked on this Earth, prayed to His Heavenly Father, and always talked about pleasing God. If you are among those who say, "Well I believe in God," then ask yourself, "Is this enough? Is believing in God enough?"

James 2:19 says, **"You believe there is one God. You do well. Even demons believe and tremble."** There will be no trembling and terrorizing demons in heaven. If there are, I do not want to go there!

To be a true Be-liever, Jesus Christ must be Savior and Lord in your heart and in your mouth. What I mean by this is, that Jesus has provided forgiveness, salvation, and deliverance for my sins as a free gift. Therefore, He wants us to acknowledge and accept Him as the new Lord of our lives. We work to please Him, follow Him, and allow Him to lead us in every decision that affects any part of our existence. It is no longer about what WE want, how WE plan, or Our needs. Jesus says in John 15:5; **"... without Me, you can do nothing."**

Going through this process will allow you to answer with a resounding "YES" to Question #1 about your 100% certainty of going to heaven. In addition, you can respond with certainty to Question #2, that the reason you should be allowed into heaven is simply because you have repented of your sins and surrendered your life to Jesus Christ as your Lord and Savior.

Therefore, the first step to Christian Discipleship is to Become a Be-liever in Jesus Christ. You believe five facts about Jesus:

1. **Who He is?**
   Jesus is the visible image of the invisible God. He came to save us from our sins. (Colossians 1:15)
2. **What He Commanded?**
   Jesus gave us a new Commandment, to love one another as He has loved us. (John 13:34-35)
3. **What He Taught?**
   Jesus taught us about the Kingdom of God, and He taught it with Authority. (Matthew 7:28-29)
4. **What He Did For You On The Cross?**
   By shedding His precious blood on the cross, Jesus made peace with God the Father for us. (Colossians 1:20)
5. **What Is He Doing For You Right Now?**
   Jesus is in heaven, sitting on the right hand of the Father, interceding on our behalf. (Romans 8:34)

I have discovered that one of the greatest, and most quoted verses found in the Bible on believing is:

> "For God so loved the world, that He gave His only begotten Son, that whoever BELIEVES in Him should not perish but have eternal life," says John 3:16.

It is important to understand that Bible-based believing is more than just mental assent. The Amplified Bible says that to believe is to obey, yield, cling, rely on, and trust in. For example, God tells you to turn down that six-figure job offer that will require a lot of time away from the family. In your current job, you can only make ends meet. That new position would resolve a lot of financial needs. However, you obey God's leading, trust his advice, and stay in your current job. Months later, you learn that the six-figure job was with a company that began huge layoffs of its employees. In your current job, you are first offered a raise and then promoted to a higher paying position.

As you can see, believing is not passive but active. For example, I can say, "I believe that if I sit down in a chair, it will give me some relief." I can say this every day, all day long. However, until I actually sit in the chair, I have not truly exhibited, Bible-based belief.

By being a Be-liever and making Jesus Christ Lord of your life, you will never, ever have to be concerned about being "stung." In fact, as be-lievers, we have these encouraging words as in 1 Corinthians 15:55-57: **"O death, where is your STING? O Hades, where is your victory? The STING of death is sin, and the strength of sin is the law. But thanks be to God, who gives us the victory through our Lord Jesus Christ."**

CONGRATULATIONS! You are now a new, born-again Be-liever. You are now affiliated with the largest family on the earth, which is the Kingdom of God.

BE A BE-LIEVER!

Five Confessions To Being A Be-Liever

1. I confess to the ABCs of Salvation in being a Be-liever and this is the first step to my Successful Christian Discipleship.
2. I confess and admit that I am a sinner and I deserve to die in my sin.
3. I confess and believe that Jesus Christ died on the cross, and forgave me of all of my sins, and I am willing to repent of all of my sins.
4. I confess that Jesus Christ is my Savior and Lord of my life.

5. I confess that I am a Be-liever, and I am saved.

PRAYER OF COMMITMENT

Heavenly Father, in the name of Jesus, I thank you for the ABCs of salvation in being a Be-liever. I understand that this is the first step to my Successful Christian Discipleship. I thank you, that although as a sinner, I deserve to die in my sins; I believe that Jesus Christ died on the cross, forgave me of all my sins, and I am willing to repent of all my sins. I thank you that Jesus Christ is my Savior and Lord of my life, and I am saved. In Jesus' Name, I pray.

Chapter 5

Step 2: Becoming A Be-longer

In Chapter 1, we discussed the first step in the process of Successful Christian Discipleship. This involves knowing our A, B and C's. In A, we **Admit** that we are sinners and that we deserve to die in our sins.

In B, we **Believe** that Jesus Christ died for, delivered, and forgave us of all our sins, and we are willing to repent of our sins. And in C, we **Confess** with our mouth, Jesus Christ as both our Lord and Savior. It is always so vital to note that, as a **Be-liever**, not only are we saved, but we should be assured of our salvation.

The beloved Apostle John writes in 1 John 5:13: **"These things I have written to you who believe in the name of the Son of God, that you may KNOW that you have eternal life and that you may continue to believe in the name of the Son of God."** After becoming a **Be-liever**, the next step in the three-step process is becoming a **Be-longer**.

Ronnie D. Simmons

As an energetic ten-year-old boy, I knew the importance and benefits of belonging to organizations. When I united with 15th Avenue Baptist Church, I was already affiliated with two youth organizations.

1. Belonging to the Cub Scouts

The first was the Cub Scouts of America. My best friend's mother who lived next door, was our Den Mother, and we had eight boys in our troop. We were expected to purchase a Cub Scout uniform which comprised of a navy blue longsleeve shirt and long pants with a belt; a blue beany cap; and a yellow scarf with a brass clip. There were opportunities we could earn patches to be worn on our uniforms and receive achievement awards for accomplishing certain tasks. We also learned how to tie a square knot and a neck-tie. In addition, we were required to purchase and read at our weekly meetings from our Cub-Scout handbook. Included in our handbook, was a copy of our Cub Scout Promise they expected us to recite at our meetings. It states:

> **"I promise to do my best**
> **To do my duty to God and my country**
> **To help other people, and**
> **To obey the Law of the Pack."**

Included were:

The Cub Scout motto - "Do your best"
The Cub Scout sign - Two separated fingers held up high (like a peace sign)
The Cub Scout salute - Two fingers together held above the brow.
The Cub Scout handshake - Handshake with two fingers extended.

During the summer when school was out, we went on a two-week camping trip to Montgomery Bell State Park, which was one of the largest parks in the State of Tennessee. During this camping trip, we went swimming and canoeing; shot bow and arrows and pellet rifles; learned how to cook fried eggs and bacon on the bottom of an empty large metal can; ate three meals a day, attended church services; sang camp songs; and performed in a talent show. This was a childhood experience that I will always cherish as a Cub Scout of America.

2. Belonging to the Salvation Army Football Team

The second organization that I belonged to at age 10, was the Salvation Army-Red Shield Jr. Pro Youth Football Team. As a football player on the team, I played both offensive tight end and defensive end.

This meant, I blocked for my teammates as we attempted to score touchdowns, and tackled my opponents to prevent them from scoring touchdowns. I was an average player with average speed, but I loved the game of Football. Although our practice field was only a few blocks away, I had to attend football practice twice a week.

After school, I would walk a half mile to practice in my football shoulder pads, pants, jersey, helmet, and football cleats. Our games were always 10-20 miles away and were played every Saturday around 10:00 a.m. This meant that I would have to be ready to leave my house around 8:00 a.m. We played hard and had a good team, but we did not win the championship. However, one of my teammates was very gifted, fast, and athletic. He pursued his football dreams by attending and playing college football for the Vanderbilt Commodores in the Southeastern Conference. He competed against top-notch players from the University of Tennessee, Alabama, Florida, and Georgia. After his college career had concluded, they drafted him in the National Football League (NFL) and he played for five years for the New England Patriots, the New York Jets, and the Cleveland Browns. Although my playing days have long been gone, I still enjoy watching and attending football games today.

My experience as a member of the Cub Scouts of America, and as a member of a youth football team, prepared me for belonging to a larger organization and being a team player. Being accepted, and belonging to these organizations as a ten-year-old, involved commitment, dedication, loyalty, and teamwork.

As a ten-year-old, I still can hear those words coming from the lips of the Pastor when he said, "Brother Ronnie, I want to extend to you the Right hand of Fellowship, you are now a member of the 15th Avenue Baptist Church." With exuberance, I graciously shook his extended hand and said; "thank you." I had belonged to the Cub Scouts of America, and to the Salvation Army Red Shield Jr. Pro Youth Football Team, but this belonging to the local church was something special that I had never experienced before.

Being a Be-longer means uniting and being actively involved with a local church. Recent research studies have revealed that only approximately 30% of professing "Christians" stated that they were actively affiliated with a local church. Even if we consider these numbers and include those who cannot attend because of chronic illnesses, conflicting work schedules, travel, or some other reasons, the low numbers are still alarming.

In listening to Be-lievers' reasonings, the major and most popular objection to becoming a Be-longer is the idea that they only need to be a Be-liever to go to heaven when they die. Technically, this is true. Belonging is not required for eternal life. However, this "fire insurance" salvation reasoning is robbing the Believer of navigating through the process of Christian Discipleship.

Two questions must be addressed.

1. **What does the Bible say or teach concerning the church?**
2. **What are the benefits of being actively involved in a local church?**

First, what does the Bible say or teach concerning the church? The Bible has much to say concerning the church. In the New Testament, from the Gospel of Matthew to the Book of Revelation, the word "church" or "churches" is mentioned nearly 100 times. Now the entire New Testament was written in the Greek language, and the word for "church" in Greek is "ecclesia." This word means "an assembly of the called-out ones."

In addressing Simon, one of His closest disciples, listened to what Jesus Christ says to him in Matthew 16:18, **"And I say to you that you are Peter, and on this rock, I will build MY CHURCH, and the gates of Hades shall not prevail against it."** Notice that the church belongs to Jesus, and not to people, and Jesus builds the church and not the people. Therefore, to fail to belong to the church is to refuse to accept what belongs to Jesus and what He builds for us. In addition, the Apostle Paul, who wrote nearly half of the 27 books in the New Testament, makes an interesting analogy between Christ and the church. In Colossians 1:18, he says, **"And He [Jesus Christ] is the head of the body, the church, who is the beginning, the firstborn from the dead, that in all things He may have the preeminence."**

In the Colossian passage, Jesus is referred to as the head, and the church is the body. Please note this. A head cannot exist without a body, nor can a body exist without a head. If you come across a headless body, please take cover, or run for your life! A person can only exist when the head is connected to the body. To say I accept a head but refuse to accept the body is ludicrous, and to say, I accept Jesus Christ as the head but refuse to accept and support his body, which is the church, is insane. If you're going to be a Be-liever, then you need to be a Be-longer!

The second question addresses the benefits of belonging to the church. Jesus, who is the builder and head of the church, would not give us something if there were no benefits. Although there are many benefits, I will list only seven of them.

Benefits of being a Be-Longer:

1. It identifies you as a genuine Be-liever. See Ephesians 2:19 and Romans 12:5.

2. It provides you with a spiritual family to support and encourage you. (See Galatians 6:1-2 and Hebrews 10:25).
3. It gives you a place to discover and use your gifts in ministry. (See 1 Corinthians 12:4-7).
4. It places you under the spiritual protection of godly leaders. (See Acts 20: 28-29).
5. It gives you the accountability you need to grow. See Ephesians 5:21.
6. The Church is called the body of Christ. Jesus is called the head. And through the body, (The Church) He carries out His will. (See Ephesians 1:20-23 and Colossians 1:17-18).
7. In Jesus' sight, spiritual family ties are even greater than blood ties. (See Mark 3:31-35).

IDENTITY

Belonging is a primary human need, after food and shelter. Having a people and place of belonging promotes a vital life. To promote sustained happiness, research confirms that income level, marriage and children, and perceived security all pale in comparison to the notion of belonging. We long to belong. We want to be part of something larger than ourselves. We often try to fit in or do things to seek approval or to feel that we belong.

The 3 B's That Do Not Sting

One reason we call the Gospel Good News is because our status changes after accepting Jesus Christ as our Lord and Savior. We are no longer "strangers and foreigners" as noted in Ephesians 2:19. We become a family, joint heirs with God's Son. We all long for a place to be, a place where we can relax, be our true selves, and be loved unconditionally. We all need a community where we belong. For everyone, a place of belonging starts with our relationship with God. To be the people of God means we are family as sisters and brothers in Christ. We belong to God's community. And belonging to Christ gives us purpose.

Look at today's standards. We have described our society as a "swipe-right culture," one that uses a popular dating app to determine the acceptability of a person with whom to socialize. When we like something at first glance, swipe right. If the moment, person, relationship, job, or community loses its appeal, we swipe left. Freedom and autonomy are the elusive promises of the swipe-right culture: The moment you're not satisfied, use your phone to find something new.

God's community is different. We learn God's truth and wisdom, healing, and empowerment of love. We embrace a unique identity as we learn the true meaning of love, forgiveness, and sharing. Christ offers security, which enables us to be established and rooted in how he has made us. We belong to Him and – in a sense – to ourselves. Not only can we become who we were, but the layers of protection that have surrounded us like shells can fall away, and true spiritual transformation can begin. In Christ, we can find true belonging, for true belonging is being simultaneously fully known and fully loved.

SPIRITUAL FAMILY

In his letter to the church in Galatia, the Apostle Paul admonishes the followers of Jesus, as they have the opportunity, they should "do good to all people, but especially to those who are of the family of Be-lievers." We often refer to a child without a family as an orphan. When we do not belong to the local church, they consider us as "spiritual orphans."

However, as followers, we are connected to the greatest family on the face of this earth; and it is called the Family of God.

As members of the family of God, we have a responsibility to assemble with one another for public worship regularly. During this time of public worship and fellowship, we can expect to be encouraged and supported, which will enable us to mature for our own spiritual development and edification.

GIFTS

When an individual accepts Jesus Christ as his or her personal Lord and Savior, one of the first gifts from the Heavenly Father is a special, supernatural spiritual gift. Although this gift is freely given, it must be discovered, used, and developed. A person cannot do God's work within the church with- out this spiritual gift, so Christian work is simply exercising one's gift(s).

God loves diversity and does not use a "cookie cutter" to stamp out the same pattern of gifts. For example, a choir is one unit, but they scatter the members throughout four sections: bass, tenor, alto, and soprano. Each section contributes to the unity of beautiful music and is more spectacular than a choir comprising only sopranos. There are many diverse members in the choir, but there is only one conductor and one choir. The Holy Spirit is the conductor of the gifts in the church and enables us to use these gifts for the glory of God.

SPIRITUAL PROTECTION

In our society today, especially in our Western culture, people view salvation as a private affair. When one accepts Jesus Christ as personal Lord and Savior, he or she creates a relationship with the Heavenly Father. The Bible refers to individuals as members of the flock of God, His sheep. Sheep are defenseless animals; they need protection if they are going to survive and flourish. The protectors are godly leaders called "shepherds," or "pastors," whom Jesus calls to protect His sheep. Sheep without a shepherd are wandering or astray and can become prey to the enemies of Christ. The shepherd's responsibility is to feed and lead, but the sheep's responsibility is to follow and swallow.

ACCOUNTABILITY

There is a familiar saying, "anything that does not grow, will eventually begin to die." One way a person can grow, develop, and mature as a Christian is to become accountable to one another through MUTUAL submission. Submission in the context of a Christian relationship includes the idea of putting someone else's needs above your own. This is not for personal benefit, but rather out of reverence for Christ.

When we serve others, we are serving the Lord.

The apostle told the church at Colosse,

> **"Whatsoever ye do, do it heartily, as to the Lord, and not unto men; Kowing that of the Lord ye shall receive the reward of the inheritance: for ye serve the Lord Christ"** Colossians 3: 23-24 KJV.

THE BODY

Our Heavenly Father makes us perfect in every good work to do His will. As members of the body, which is the church, Jesus is working in us. In addition, Jesus injects new confidence in the follower that if the person asks anything according to His will, He hears us, and we know that if He hears us, we know that whatever we ask, we have the petitions desired of him.

FAMILY TIES

Jesus' family can be found where the words of Jesus and the will of God are cherished and obeyed. By no means is this meant to slight those with whom we have biological ties. However, it is a reminder that our family relationship in the sight of God is stronger than even our ties to our physical families. Jesus' family is the forever family of people who love Him, obey Him, and allow His Holy Spirit to lead, guide, and empower them.

It is so vital for you as a Be-liever to find a local church in which you can become a Be-longer. However, belonging to any church won't do. Seek a church of the Lord Jesus Christ that preaches and teaches the Word of God, loves people, and shares a

vision of 1) Exalting the Savior; 2) Equipping the Saints for the work of the Ministry; and 3)
Evangelizing the Sinner.

Belong to a church of the Lord Jesus Christ with purposes that include: 1) Evangelism, 2) Worship, 3) Fellowship, 4) Discipleship, and 5) Ministry. Belong to a church of the Lord Je- sus Christ that exhibits excellence, provides encouragement, and shows effectiveness. Belong to a church of the Lord Jesus Christ in which He builds, and He is the head. If you do, you will not have to be concerned about being "stung," because you are covered and protected in the body of Christ.

Become A BE-LONGER Today!

Five Confessions to Becoming a Be-longer

1. I confess that I am a Be-longer to the church of the Lord Jesus Christ, which is the next step to Successful Christian Discipleship.

2. I confess that as a Be-longer to the church of the Lord Je- sus Christ, I have been called out of the world system into an assembly of people who share in the Kingdom of God system.

3. I confess that as a Be-longer, Jesus Christ is the head, and I am a part of His body which is the church.

4. I confess that as a Be-longer to the church, because Jesus Christ is the builder and head of the church, by faith, I receive, and walk in all the benefits.

5. I confess that I am affiliated with a church with a vision that includes exalting the Savior, equipping the Saints, and evangelizing the Sinner.

PRAYER OF COMMITMENT

Father, in the name of Jesus, I thank you that I am a Be-longer to the church of the Lord Jesus Christ, which is the next step to Successful Christian Discipleship. I thank you that I have been called out of the world system into an assembly of people who share in the Kingdom of God system. Jesus Christ is my head, and I am a part of His body, which is the church. I thank you that Jesus Christ is the builder and head of the church. I walk in all the benefits. His vision includes exalting the Savior, equipping the saints, and evangelizing the Sinner. In Jesus' Name, I pray. Amen.

Chapter 6

Step 3: Being a Be-Comer

*T*he previous chapters focused on two of the steps required for Successful Christian Discipleship being a Be-liever and a Be-longer. The last step of the three-step process, I must admit, is the most challenging. However, being a Be-comer can be the most rewarding and fulfilling.

You may ask, "What am I becoming?" And the answer is "becoming more like Jesus." Yes, becoming more like Jesus is the third and final step to successful Christian Discipleship.

When I was first introduced to this final step of becoming more like Jesus, my initial response was, "No

Ronnie D. Simmons

way, this is impossible because we all know that no one can become like Jesus!" Again, this is the most challenging, but the most rewarding and fulfilling of all the steps.

Webster's Dictionary defines **"become"** as to come or grow to be. Therefore, we can say that a **Be-comer** is a **Be-liever,** and a **Be-longer** who has decided to grow to be a Be-comer like Jesus Christ.

The definition may spark these three questions:

1) **What does the Bible say and teach about becoming more like Jesus?**
2) **Is it possible to become more like Jesus?**
3) **What are the benefits of becoming more like Jesus?**

Let us investigate:

1) **What does the Bible say and teach about becoming more like Jesus?**

The Bible has much to say about us becoming more like Jesus. As I mentioned in my dedication, I dedicate this book to both of my parents, Mr. Ernest and Mrs. Mattie Simmons who have since been deceased. My mother, transitioned in 1972 when I was only 15 years old. I was very close to my mother; however, our time spent together was cut short in my teenage years. She was very compassionate and taught me to treat people the way I wanted to be treated. She always put others first before herself. She was only 54 when she passed away.

After her passing, I began appreciating my father more and more. While growing up, and while my mother was living, my father worked six days a week, twelve hours a day.

Because he was an excellent chef, it was required that he had to work on Sundays at the Country Club in Belle Meade, so he only went to church with us, when he was on vacation. However, after my mother passed, my father's hours were reduced, and he retired shortly thereafter. After his retirement, I was able to spend more time with him, and unknowingly I mimicked some of his ways.

Family members told me I would stand, swing my arms, and walk just like my father. I was becoming more and more like him, because he had become the most important man in my life, and I wanted to be like my father. I wanted to please him in everything that I did. I once met an older man who used to work with my father in the Restaurant business.

My father's nickname at the time was "Unk". When I was sixteen, this man hired me as a busboy at a Restaurant where the entertainers, musicians, and movie stars would visit regularly when they came to Nashville. After a short time of employment, he started calling me "little Unk", because he stated I reminded him of my father. Although my father has been deceased since 1992, I still have a relative who because she states I look and carry myself so much like my father, refers to me as "little Ernest." The greatest compliment my father made to me before he passed away was, "Ronnie, I am so proud of you as my son."

No, I am not Ernest Simmons, and we are two different people. However, just like I hoped to become more like my father, it should be the desire of every Believer to become more like Jesus.

Becoming More Like Jesus

Please note that I did not say we are to be Jesus. No, there is only one Jesus who has lived on this Earth. And the thirty-three years he walked this Earth, He was fully human, capable of pains, temptations, and suffering, and yet fully divine as the Son of God and God Incarnate. He was sinless but died and received humanity's punishment for the sins of the world so that he could be resurrected to provide eternal life to those who believe in Him. There never has been, nor will there ever be another Jesus. He is the one and only Jesus Christ of Nazareth.

Let's examine the first question. What does the Bible say and teach about becoming more like Jesus? Listen to what the Apostle Paul says to the Christians in Romans 8:29 in the New Living Translation: **"For God** knew his people in advance, and he chose them to **BECOME LIKE HIS SON** so that his Son would be the firstborn, among many brothers and sisters."

Here is what the beloved disciple John says to the Be-lievers and Be-longers in 1 John 3:2 (NLT).

"Dear friends, we are already God's children, but he has not yet shown us what we will be like when Christ appears. But we do know that we will BE LIKE HIM, for we will see him as he really is."

We must understand that God's goal in this three-step process to Successful Christian Discipleship is to make us become like Jesus Christ. As we become more like him, we will discover our true selves, the person we were created to be.

2) Is It Possible To Become More Like Jesus?

Next, you may ask; is it possible to become more like Jesus? Yes, eventually. The Christian life is a process of becoming more like Christ. This process will not be complete until we see Jesus Christ face to face. However, knowing that this is our ultimate destiny should motivate us to purify ourselves

Here are four ways to become more like Jesus Christ:

1. Read The Bible And Obey The Teachings Of Jesus Christ.

Make Bible reading a part of each day. Select a time or part of the day and the time you have to devote to it–5 minutes, 10 minutes, 30 minutes, one or two hours. The Bible is a collection of literary works written by 40 different authors over 1,500 years ago. Christians believe that the 66 books divided into the Old and New Testaments that make up the Bible are the written word of God and that God inspired and directed each author. The Bible is the ultimate authority on how Christians should conduct themselves and live their lives as followers of Christ.

2. Study The Life Of Jesus Christ On Earth Through The Four Gospels: Matthew, Mark, Luke, And John.

The term gospel means "Good News." The Bible declares good news about Jesus Christ and His marvelous salvation. These four books of the New Testament tell this story of Jesus Christ's salvation for lost man and, therefore, are referred to as the gospels. Each book expresses a particular view of Jesus–as a King, a servant, as man, and as God. Understanding the different perspectives of Jesus is like appreciating our own roles in life. A woman can be a wife, mother, sister, aunt, meal preparer, housekeeper, launderer, and soccer mom. A man can be a father, son, husband, wage earner, technician, little league coach, or discipliner. I hope you understand the point here.

3. Spend Quality Time In Prayer.

What is Prayer? Prayer is loving communication with God who is our Heavenly Father. Prayer is the expression of our inner spiritual needs. Through prayer, we can find strength of spirit, guidance, wisdom, joy, and inner peace.

Some important aspects of prayer include A.C.T.S.

A: Adoration - We adore our Heavenly Father by acknowledging Him and by telling him how much we appreciate Him as the source of our lives.

C: Confession - We confess and repent of our sins and shortcomings and ask for forgiveness. In addition, we confess the promises of God made to us in His word.

T: Thanksgiving - We thank Him for His grace, mercy, love, and compassion. We thank Him for the Ministry of Jesus Christ and the work of the Holy Spirit in our lives.

S: Supplication - We ask Him to daily supply our needs as well as the needs of others.

Prayer is not a monologue, but a dialogue. Therefore, there must be quality, uninterrupted time set aside in our day, to talk to and with God, and to listen to Him speak to us.

In Ephesians 5:18, the Apostle Paul says, **"Do not be drunk with wine, but be filled with the Holy Spirit."** But what does this mean? This is not a suggestion but a command for followers of Jesus Christ to live continually under the influence of the Holy Spirit by allowing the Word of God to control us; dying to self and surrendering to God's will. Being filled with the Spirit involves fellowshipping with the Lord Jesus and allowing His words to dominate everything we say or do.

4) Love People, The Same Way Jesus Loved Us.

This new commandment that Jesus gives to His followers fulfills the old commandment of **"Love the Lord God with all of your heart, mind, strength, and soul"** Deuteronomy 6:5 KJV. This is an old Mosaic commandment under the law, that has set the stage for us as God's creation to love Him.

In Matthew 22:39-40, Jesus says, **"And the second is like it: 'You shall Love your neighbor as yourself.' On these two commandments hang all the law and the Prophets"** (NKJV).

In John 13:34-35, He says, **"A new commandment, I give unto you, that you love one another as I have loved you, that you love one another. By this, will all know that you are my disciples, if you have love one to another"** (KJV).

Let me explain the essence of this new commandment. The above scripture can be found in Luke 10:27. This scripture which is often mistaken as a commandment of Jesus, is actually stated by a Jewish lawyer, (a scholar of the Law of Moses) who wanted to test Jesus by asking him the question; **"Teacher, what must I do to inherit eternal life?"** Jesus, response to him was; **"What is written in the law?"** (The Law of Moses) What is your reading of it? And this lawyer's response to Jesus' question was "Love the Lord God with all of your heart, mind, strength, and soul, and love your neighbor as yourself." As Christians, we are not under the Law, but under Grace.

The Apostle John records these insightful words in John 1:17 when he said, **"For the law was given through Moses, but grace and truth came through Jesus Christ"** (NKJV). No one could keep the law. It was based on your performance which meant, that if you did good, you received good results, however, if you did evil, you were punished.

Under grace, it is not based upon what you do, it is based upon what Jesus has already done for you on the Cross at Calvary when he forgave and delivered you from all your past, present, and future sins. This is His part. Our part is to receive everything He has done for us, by Faith.

3) What Are The Benefits Of Becoming More Like Jesus?

We can see some of those benefits in the promise Jesus leaves us in John 14:12 in the New Living Translation: **"The truth is, anyone who believes in me will do the same works I have done, and even greater works, because I am going to be with the Father"** (NLT). Can you imagine doing greater works than Jesus? However, the greater works that Jesus is speaking of here are in reference to the disciples working in the power of the Holy Spirit and carrying out the Good News of the Kingdom of God throughout the whole world (on a larger scale than Jesus did as one person).

When you decide to become more like Jesus Christ, you will never have to be concerned with being "stung."

Five Confessions of Being a Be-comer

1. I confess that being a Be-comer leads to Successful Christian Discipleship.
2. I confess that becoming more like Jesus, though probably the most challenging, is the most rewarding of all the steps to Successful Christian Discipleship.
3. I confess that as I become more like Jesus Christ, I will discover my true self and the person I was created to be.
4. I confess that the process of becoming more like Jesus Christ will not be complete until I see Him face to face.
5. I confess that becoming more like Jesus will allow the working of the power of the Holy Spirit in my life, and the carrying out of the Good News of the Kingdom of God throughout the world.

PRAYER OF COMMITMENT

Father, in the name of Jesus, I thank you that you've made the step "Becoming more like Jesus" the most challenging, yet the most rewarding of all the steps to Successful Christian Discipleship. I thank you that as I become more like Jesus Christ, I will discover my true self, the person I was created to be. However, I will not be complete until I see Him face to face. I thank you that becoming more like Jesus will allow the working of the power of the Holy Spirit in my life, and the carrying out of the Good News of the Kingdom of God throughout the world. In Jesus' name, I pray. Amen.

PART 3

Chapter 7

Summary

I began this book, *3 B's That Do Not Sting,* by raising this question; "Have you ever been stung by a honey- bee or have you heard what it feels like"? The most popular response is; "It hurts, it causes swelling, itching, and other allergic reactions." One sting caused all of this. The lesson learned is, if possible, stay away from bees, and if you must be around them, make sure you do not agitate them and you are wearing protective clothing.

As a follower of Jesus, I want you to respect bees, and learn from them, but do not fear them. The Apostle Paul writes to his son in the ministry these astounding words. **"For God has not given us, the spirit of fear,**

but of love, power, and a sound mind" (2 Timothy 1:7 KJV).

You may ask "What about their sting"? My response is for you to take your focus off the bee and the sting, and become excited about what Jesus Christ your Lord and Savior has done for you. 2000 years ago, he took the sting out of death and robbed the grave of the Victory. Therefore, I raise my voice with the Apostle Paul in glorious triumph with this thought-provoking, mind-boggling, and inquisitive question when asked the rhetorical question; **"O death, where is thy sting"? O Grave where is thy victory?"**

The Valiant Triumph of Victory in the 3 Bs

These 3 Bs Do Not Sting!

Becoming a Be-liever

As a Be-liever, you have nothing to fear because you believe in the Name of the Lord Jesus Christ, a name that is above every name; you are now saved, forgiven, and delivered from your sins. You have the assurance and confidence of your salvation both now and in eternity. Hallelujah!

Becoming a Be-longer

As a Be-longer, you have nothing to fear because you belong to the church of the Lord Jesus Christ; you have a spiritual family of like-minded brothers and sisters, which means you are now connected to His body, and He is the head which will give you instructions for daily living. Hallelujah!

Being a Be-comer

As a Be-Comer, you have nothing to fear because you have the mind of Christ; you are being conformed to His image, and each day you are becoming more like Him. You represent Jesus and the same Holy Spirit that resided in Him, now resides in you. Hallelujah!

Daily Scriptural Prayers to Protect you from the "Sting" of sin.

As a Be-liever

Father, I thank you that according to John 3:16, because you so loved me, that you gave your only begotten Son for me, that as I believe in Jesus, I will not perish, but I shall have everlasting life. In the Name of Jesus. Amen.

*F**ather*, I thank you that according to Romans 10:9, because I have confessed with my mouth the Lord Jesus, and have believed in my heart, that you have raised Jesus Christ from the grave, I am now saved. In the Name of Jesus. Amen.

*F**ather*, I thank you that according to Ephesians 2:8-9, because of your grace, I have been saved through faith in the Lord Jesus Christ, and it was not of myself. It was a gift of God, not of my works, therefore, I have nothing to boast about. In the Name of Jesus. Amen.

As a Be-longer

*F**ather*, I thank you that I belong to the church of the Lord Jesus Christ, and according to Ephesians 1:2023, the church is the body of Christ, and through the church, Jesus carries out His will for my life. In the Name of Jesus. Amen.

*F**ather*, I thank you that I belong to the church of the Lord Jesus Christ. According to Galatians 6:1-2, the church is my spiritual family and it is the place where I will be supported and encouraged by my spiritual brothers and sisters. In the Name of Jesus. Amen.

Father, I thank you that I belong to the church of the Lord Jesus Christ. According to Hebrews 13:17, I will submit to my godly spiritual leaders, because they are constantly watching over my soul. In the Name of Jesus. Amen.

As a Be-comer

Father, I thank you that according to 2 Corinthians 5:17, I am a new creation in Christ Jesus. Old things have passed away, and behold all things have become new. In Jesus' Name. Amen.

Father, I thank you that according to Romans 8:29, I have been predestined to conform to the image of Jesus and to become just like Him. I have the mind of Christ, and I represent Him. In Jesus' Name. Amen.

Father, I thank you that according to 1 John 2:6, as I abide, obey, and remain in the teachings and instructions of Jesus, I will possess the same Holy Spirit's presence and power that abided in Jesus. In Jesus' Name. Amen.

Chapter 8

Resources

I pray that this book "3 B's That Do Not Sting;" has been a blessing to you. If it has, then I would encourage you to pick up a copy for your family members, friends, or a new or seasoned brother or sister in Christ. They can also use this book as a tool for your bible study, or small group fellowship.

To further your spiritual enrichment and development as a:

BE-Liever
BE-Longer
BE-comer

The following are some reading materials and scripture-based prayers that will help you on your spiritual journey.

1. Books

These books cover a range of topics from foundational beliefs and evidence from Christianity to deepening one's relationship with God through His Son Jesus Christ and understanding His purpose for our lives. They can provide valuable insights and guidance as you become a BE-Liever, a BE-Longer, and a BE-Comer.

Evangelism Explosion by Dr. D James Kennedy

This is more than a book, for Dr. Kennedy introduces this resource as a valuable training manual on how churches will learn a biblically based method for sharing the Gospel. In addition, Dr. Kennedy provides many motivational tools for "on the job" training on how to share Jesus with others, as well as developing new believers.

The Gospel According to Jesus by John MacArthur

John MacArthur's well-known book addresses the idea of "easy believe-ism" in churches and encourages

Christians to evaluate their commitment to Jesus by looking at their fruit.

The Triumphant Church by Kenneth Hagin

In this classic edition, Bro. Kenneth E. Hagin, who many consider the father of the "word of faith" movement, introduces the believer to the difference between oppression, obsession, and possession, and discusses various ways believers can give Satan access into their lives. This book will reveal how to defeat Satan in your life so you can live in the victory God intended for every believer in Jesus Christ.

The Jesus I Never Knew by Philip Yancey

Phillip Yancey in this informative and inspirational book, offers a new perspective on the life, the work, the teachings, the miracles, and the death, burial, and resurrection of Jesus Christ. Moreover, Yancey exposes the identity of Jesus Christ and the motivation behind His arrival.

Lord, Teach Me How To Love by Creflo A. Dollar

In this challenging and compelling book, Dr. Dollar explains that closeness to God is not based upon our good works, but is based on cultivating a true and loving relationship with our Heavenly Father. Dr. Dollar invites us to discover the true love that only comes from experiencing the love of God through fellowshipping with His Son Jesus Christ and following His example.

3. Scripture-based prayers related to the 3 B's That Do Not Sting Be-Coming a Be-Liever

My friend, one question you may grapple with is; "Why is it so difficult for me to decide to become a believer and accept Jesus Christ as my Savior and Lord?" Beloved, do not feel alone, for many others have asked this same question. However, there are two reasons you may feel this way:

1) Satan, who the bible refers to as "the father of lies" and "the prince of darkness", hates God and is the enemy of God and His Righteousness. And He will do anything and everything in his power to thwart the plan of God and to keep you and me from accepting Jesus Christ as your personal Lord and Savior.

2) It is very difficult to fathom in your mind the idea of a Holy and Righteous God, loving you so much, that He would allow His own sinless Son to die on the cross and to forgive you for all the wrong decisions and choices, you have made in your life.

If you feel this way or have similar feelings or questions, I would like for you to pray out loud these prayers of faith.

My Confession Prayer

Father, in the Name of Jesus Christ of Nazareth, the Son of the Living God, I believe that it is your desire that I accept Jesus Christ as my personal Lord and Savior. Therefore, I renounce Satan who is your enemy, and my enemy from trying to influence my mind and my thinking. You said in your word according to Matthew 16:19; **"whatever, I bind on earth, shall be bound in heaven, and whatever I lose on earth shall be loosed in heaven."** I take authority over Him, I bind Him, and He is under my feet. Now, Father, I thank you that according to Colossians 1:13; I have been delivered from the power of darkness and have been translated into the Kingdom of Jesus Christ and His love for me on the cross. By faith, I choose Jesus, I accept Jesus, and I surrender my life to Jesus. Thank you for saving my life. In Jesus' Name, I pray. Amen.

My Confession Prayer

Father, I come to You in the Name of Jesus Christ of Nazareth, the Son of the Living God. Father, I must admit that it is difficult for my mind to comprehend why You would allow Your only Son who was sinless to die on the cross, to forgive me and save me from all of my sins. I have said many wrong things that I should not have said, and done many other evil things, that I should not have done. And you still provided salvation for me. However, according to your word in Titus 3:4-6, you said;

"But when the kindness and the love of God appeared [to me]; not by works of righteousness which I have done, but according to His mercy, He saved me, through the washing of regeneration and renewing of the Holy Spirit, whom He poured out on me abundantly through Jesus Christ my Savior." I now accept Jesus Christ as my Lord and Savior, not based on what I have done, but based upon Your love for me and what Jesus Christ did for me on the cross. He took my sins away. By faith, I choose Jesus, I accept Jesus, and I surrender my life to Jesus. Thank you for saving my life. I am a BE-liever. In Jesus' Name, I pray. Amen.

BE-Coming a Be-Longer

My friend, you may have been contemplating for a while the issue of whether to become a Be-longer to a local church. You may have had a terrible experience with the last church you belonged to, and that awful taste of how you were treated is still in your mouth. You're not alone in feeling this way; many people are still struggling with the same issue. Even I know how you feel; for I have felt the same way; but this is what I have found. Allow me to speak candidly to you. Whenever I have to make an important decision, one factor I consider is "What are the benefits for me?" Here, you must ask yourself this question, "Why would a loving God tell me to do something without sharing and providing me with the benefits?" What benefits does it provide?

If this applies to you, and you are looking for the benefits of Be-longing to a local church, then I would encourage you to pray out loud, this prayer of faith.

Ronnie D. Simmons

A Be-Longer's Prayer

"Father, I come to You in the Name of Jesus Christ of Nazareth, the Son of the Living God. Your word says in Ephesians 1:20-21; **"That You are able to do EXCEEDINGLY, ABUNDANTLY, above all that I ask or think, according to the power [of love of Jesus Christ] which works in me. To Him be glory in the CHURCH by Christ Jesus to all generations, forever and ever."**

Thank you, Father, for the benefit of loving me, and going far over and above my personal request and prayers as I honor, glorify, and praise the Name of Jesus. Jesus, I receive this benefit by faith, because You are my head, and I belong to Your Body, which is the CHURCH. I am a Be-longer. In Jesus' Name, I pray. Amen.

Being a Be-Comer

Growing up as a teenager in the 70s, when someone would make an outlandish statement that appears to sound so ridiculous that my mind could not comprehend, I would respond with a loud;

"WHAT! NO WAY!" My friend, this is how I almost responded when I was instructed to BE-come more like Jesus Christ. To become like the one who fasted for 40 days and 40 nights; one who turned water into wine, walked on water, opened blinded eyes, healed the sick, raised the dead, and fed over 20,000 people with a two-piece fish dinner? And I am expected to BE-come more like Him?

Remember, my friend, Jesus only did what His Father told Him to do and what was pleasing in His sight. This obedience is only possible for us when we spend more time in fellowship with Jesus through His words and teachings, and as we are led by the Holy Spirit.

My friend, if you would like to become more like Jesus in conforming to His image, having the Mind of Christ, and walking as He walked, then I ask you to pray out loud this prayer of faith.

Ronnie D. Simmons

My Be-Comer's Prayer

"Father, I come to You in the Name of Jesus Christ of Nazareth, the Son of the Living God. Father, I must admit that in my flesh it seems that it is totally impossible to become more like Jesus, however, I do not walk by my physical senses; I walk by faith. According to the words of Jesus in John 14:12- 14, He says; **"Most assuredly, I say to you, he who believes in Me, the works that I do he will do also; and greater works than these will he do, because I go to My Father. And whatever you ask in My name, that I will do, that the Father may be glorified in the Son. If you ask anything in My name, I will do it."** I thank You that I am becoming more like Jesus when I love others the way He loved me; overcome temptations by speaking the word of God; and by doing those things that are pleasing in Your sight. I realize that I can only accomplish these desires as I walk in obedience to You, and allow the Holy Spirit to lead, guide, and direct my life. I thank you that by faith, I am becoming more like Jesus every day of my life. I am a BE-comer. In Jesus' Name, I pray. Amen."

In the tapestry of Be-Coming, we are called to embrace the joy of not being stung, and being shielded by the love and grace of Almighty God. It is a joy that transcends circumstances, a joy that transforms lives, and a joy that radiates from the heart of Jesus Christ when He loved me on the cross.

In closing, we invite you to heed the clarion and passionate call to BEE-come a Believer, to BEE-long to a local church, and BEE-come more like Jesus. Do not allow the swarm of life's distractions to deter you from embracing the truth. Jesus prayed for us when He asked His Father in John 17: 17, "**Sanctify them with Your truth, your word is truth.**" The joy of not being stung awaits a joy that extends far beyond this earthly realm. Step into the abundant, amazing, and anointed life that God has prepared for you, and let your heart overflow with gratitude, thanksgiving, and praise.

Remember, the choice is yours. Will you choose the path of BEE-coming or risk the dangers of a life without Jesus Christ of Nazareth, the Son of the Living God? The swarm awaits you.

BEE Blessed in Jesus!

PRAYER FOR SALVATION AND BAPTISM

IN THE HOLY GHOST

Prayer for Salvation

Most Gracious Heavenly Father, I come to You right now in the precious Name of Your Son Jesus Christ. I admit that I am a sinner and I deserve to die for my sins. I believe that Jesus died on the cross for my sins, he was raised on the third day, and He is alive right now. I repent of all of my sins and I surrender myself totally and completely to You. I confess Jesus Christ as my Savior and Lord. I ask you to change me right now. You said in Your Word that whosoever shall call upon the Name of the Lord. As my new Lord and Savior from this day forward, I dedicate my life to serving Him. Thank you for saving me in Jesus' Name.

Prayer for Baptism in the Holy Ghost

Dear Jesus, you said, "How much more shall your heavenly Father give the Holy Spirit to those who ask Him." I ask of you Jesus to fill me with Your Holy Spirit and with power. I step in the fullness, ability, and authority that I desire in Your Name. Jesus, just as I confess with my mouth that You are my Lord, I now confess that I am a Spirit-filled Christian. As I yield my will, my spirit, my tongue, and my vocal cords, I expect to speak in tongues as the Holy Spirit gives me utterance. I thank you by faith for baptizing me in the Holy Ghost and for my new prayer language.

ABOUT AUTHOR

Ronnie D. Simmons is the Senior Pastor and founder of House of Faith Christian Center, a word of faith, non-denominational, multi-racial church located in Smyrna, Tennessee. He has been in the Ministry since 1980 but was directed by the Holy Spirit to begin House of Faith Christian Center in 1992. He is also the founder and President of Ronnie Simmons Ministries (RSM) and Compassion in Action Ministries. (CIAM)

Pastor Simmons is the host of a daily international inspirational devotional for men called; "Man of Up", which can be viewed on his Facebook page. In addition, he hosts a Mid-week teleconference Bible Study entitled; "Hour of Power."

Born and raised in Nashville Tennessee, Pastor Simmons is a graduate of the University of Tennessee and Victory Bible Training Center in Nashville. He has carried his message of "Trained well, to Serve Well" of Christian Discipleship to as far as the country of the Democratic Republic of Congo in Central Africa; where he is the spiritual father of the pastor of the Jasper Stone Evangelical Church in Kinshasa.

The 3 B's That Do Not Sting

One of Pastor Simmons' greatest achievements is being a ten-gallon plus blood donor to the American Red Cross to help save lives. He believes that since Jesus Christ shed his precious blood to save his life for him 2000 years ago, he ought to donate blood to help save the lives of others. He is the husband of Terrie Simmons, and together they pastor the House of Faith Christian Center. The couple has two adult children, Joshua (Sierra) and Jessica (Vince), and five grandchildren, Essence, Exavier, Kaleb, Kannon, Shiloh, and his bonus child, Levi.

Ronnie Simmons Ministries (RSM) is the outreach ministry of House of Faith Christian Center. Its vision is to:
1) Exalt the Savior;
2) Equip the Saints and
3) Evangelize the sinner for the Kingdom of God.

Send us your prayer request, praise report, or testimonies of how this Book has impacted your life.
Contact us: Ronnie Simmons Ministries
    P.O. Box 985, Smyrna, Tennessee 37167
www.houseoffaithchristiancenter.org
    Tel: (615) 223-0420

Follow us on Facebook at House of Faith Christian Center Smyrna

Ronnie D. Simmons

THE END

Made in United States
Orlando, FL
30 October 2023